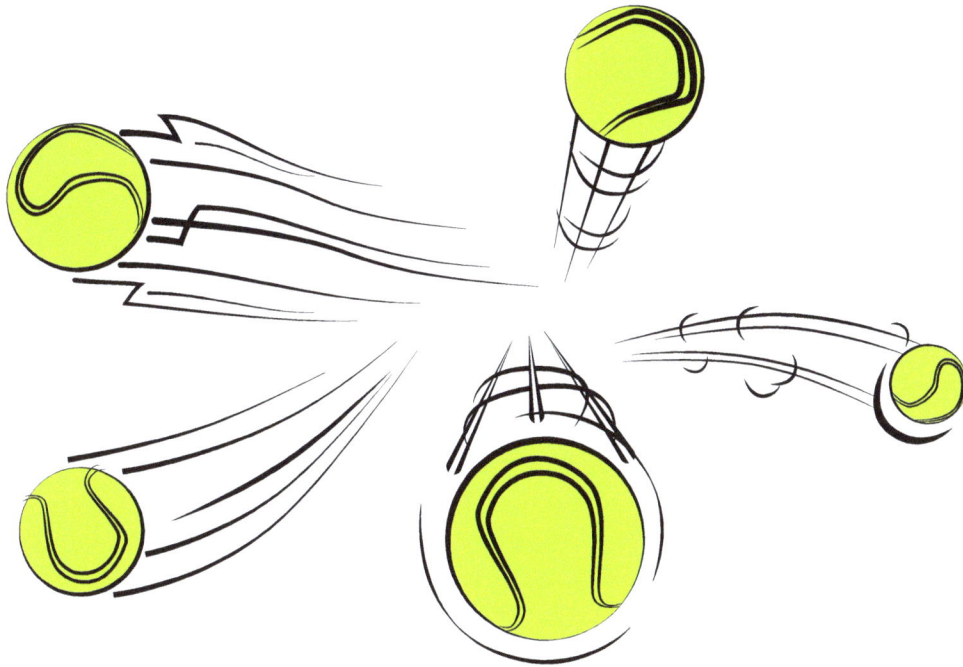

Ode to Tennis

Written by Barbara Wyatt

Illustrations by Mario Barrera

Wild Creek Publishing Group,
P.O. Box 2061, Tacoma WA 98401
www.iKnowTennis.com
2nd Edition June 2017

Wyatt, Barbara
Ode to Tennis / by Barbara Wyatt
Summary: Humorous poem about a tennis player's efforts to learn
the game of tennis during a lesson with tennis instructor.

ISBN-10:0-9984466-3-7
ISBN-13:978-0-9984466-3-9

1. Tennis – Humor 2. Tennis – poetry.
3. Sports – humor 4. Sports – Sociological aspects - humor

Dedication

Greg and Cindy Smith

Eric Drew

Rick Schroll

Betsy Purpura

Ryan Paul

Michael Parretta

Tracey Ann Ferry

Josh Pinyerd

Brian Nash

Zuzana Brogdon

Vern Ball

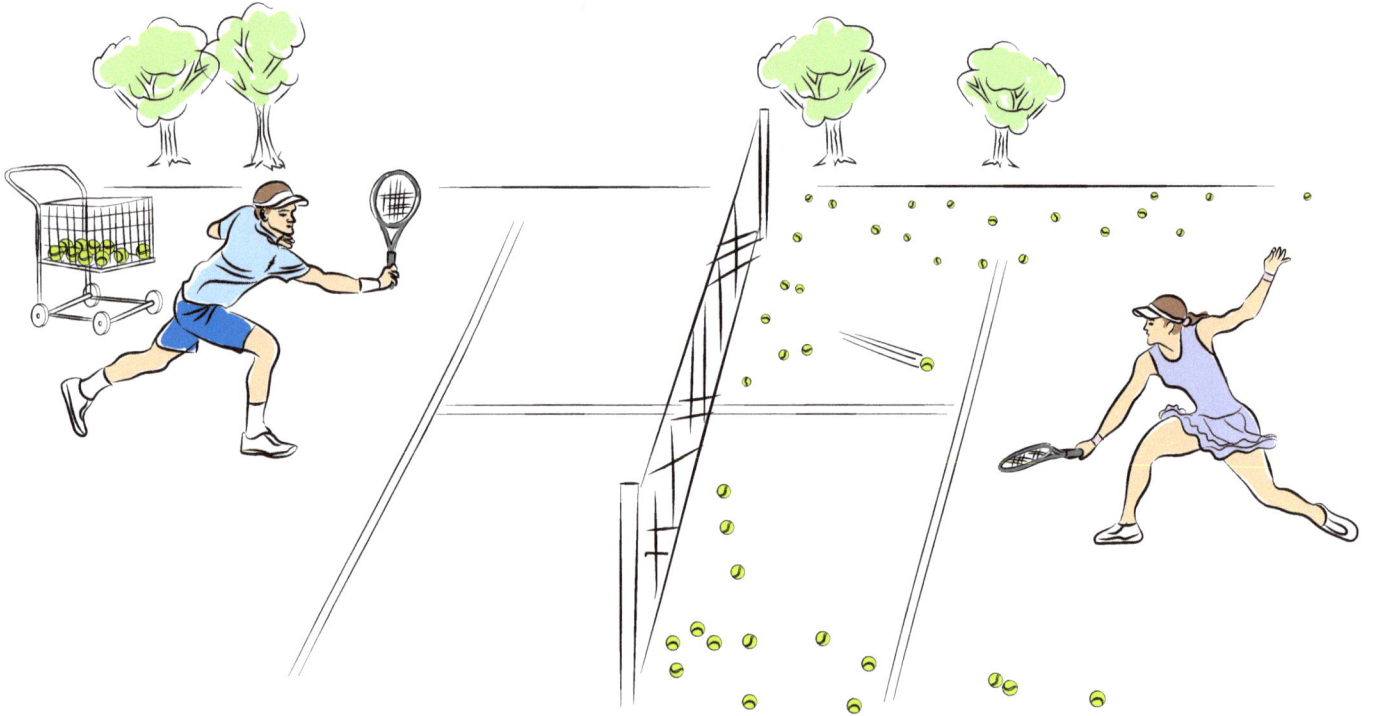

Forehand, backhand,
Inside-out shots and more,
"Racquet in front," the old Pro yells,
"Make that ball soar!"

I whip it, I flip it,
The ball flies deep with spin.
No doubt Rafael Nadal
Is my identical twin.

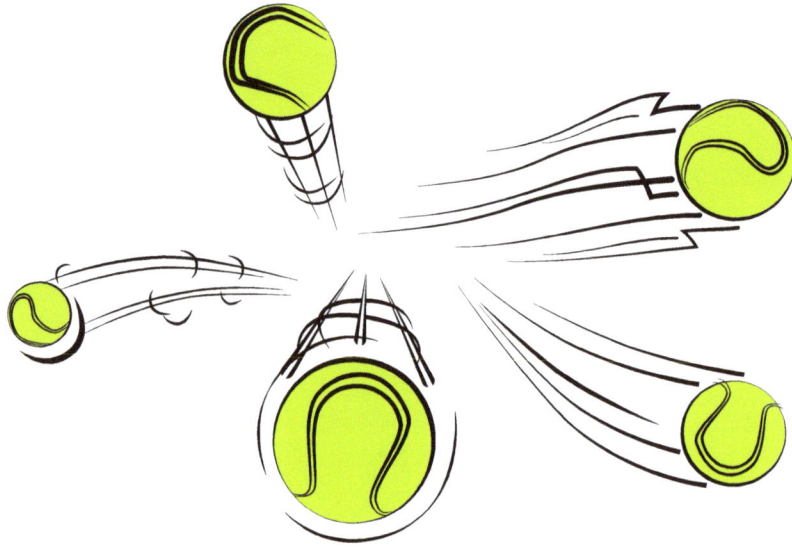

The Pro feeds me hundreds of balls
As I laugh and sweat.
I chase after each and every one,
And hit them over the net!

I run cross court
then back again.
My shots are so good
I'll be famous on ESPN!

But the Pro played in college,
Then on to the circuit for fun
While I'm a late starter
Who is clearly outdone.

"Follow through!" he cries.
But all I can muster is a sneer,
"Bend your knees!" he adds,
So I scoot lower and sing out a cheer.

Watch the ball.

Turn your shoulder.

Split step!

Follow through!

Step into the shot.

Hit underneath the ball.

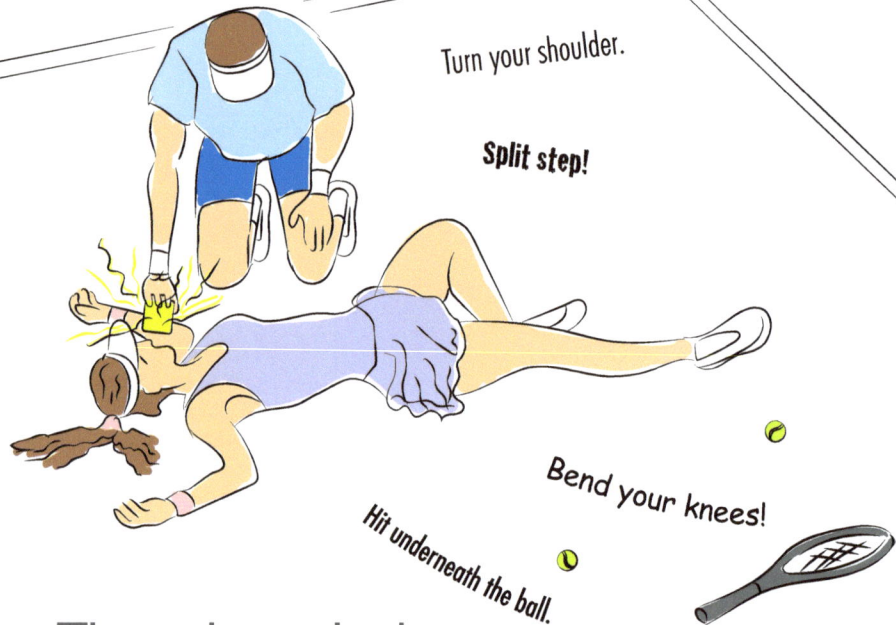

Bend your knees!

Throughout the lesson,
The Pro shows me my faults.
Only once (I promise!) did he resurrect me
With a bag of smelling salts.

I chase the ball in tournaments,
I compete in the USTA,
Yet my strokes leave players laughing.
I'm more comical than Tina Fey!

ESPN won't *ever* feature me.
I'm an old, "casual" player.

No matter how much I practice my serve and my lobs,
My hair goes grayer and grayer.

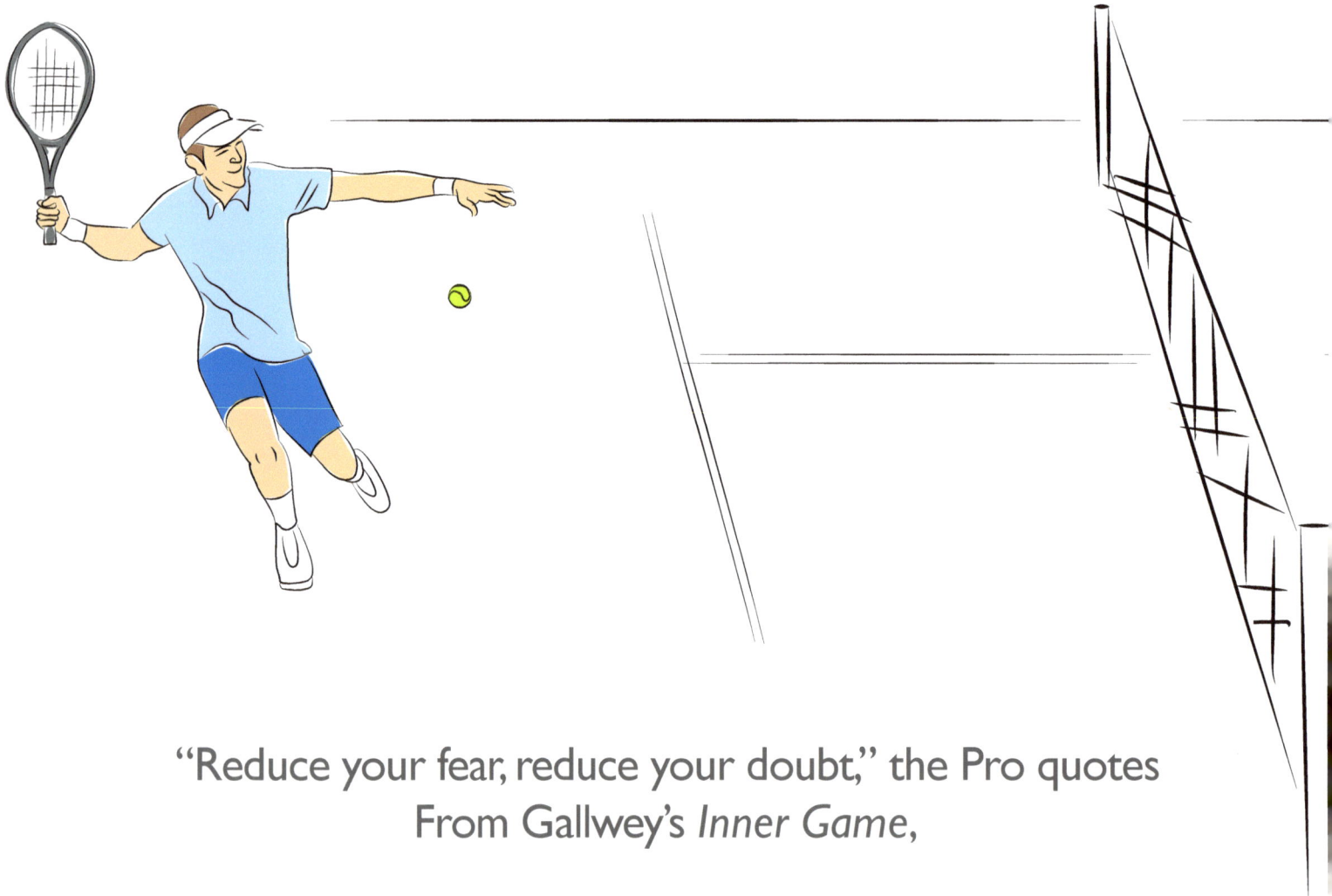

"Reduce your fear, reduce your doubt," the Pro quotes
From Gallwey's *Inner Game*,

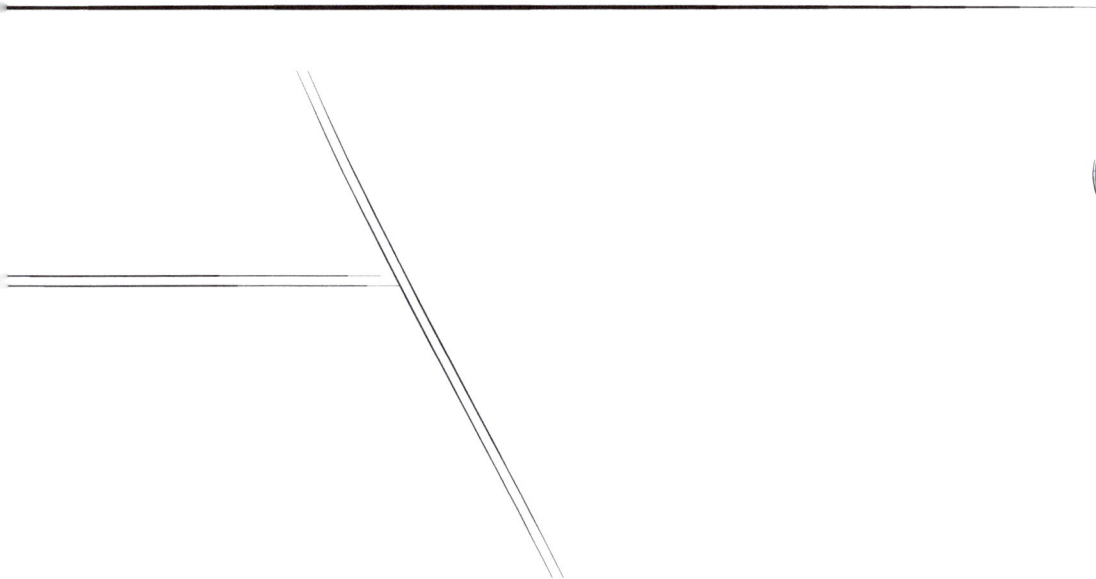

So I split-step and balance on my toes,
And take a steady, tranquil aim.

The Pro's return is deep and wide,
So I stretch, stretch, *stretch* my racquet out,
And though my return rips cross-court,
Still, I am filled with doubt.

Yet there it is! My ball landed true
With a sharp angle to admire!
I've caught the Pro on his heels,
My top-spin sending the ball higher and higher!

The Pro's college matches are too far past.
Tennis teaching certificates be damned!
It's *me*, the late start player,
Who made that ball go WHAM!

He laughs! He applauds!
"I knew you could do it!" he says
Then he feeds me more balls.
Top-spin backhands is what I will hit.

I grip my racquet and whisper a little prayer
and smack the ball into the air
Where it soars past the lines and into the blue,
Landing…who knows where!

"Bend your knees!" the Old Pro yells.
Oh, how many times have I heard this before?
But "Worry not!" he adds. "We'll fix that stroke.
You won't do that anymore."

"For your match drawing near," the Pro advises,
"*You* be the pace setter."
I nod and affirm.
"Next lesson, my Pro, I promise I'll do better."

Mario Barrera, Illustrator
Mario Barrera, formerly a musician, is a graphic designer, Illustrator and soccer lover. In addition to design, he loves soccer, banging on the drums/percussion or playing the guitar with friends or family. He can be reached by email at tingamio@yahoo.com

Barbara Wyatt, Poet
Barbara Wyatt is a writer, photographer, USTA official and mobile app developer for iKnowTennis!, the tennis rules app. Wyatt discovered the game of tennis about 10 years ago and is striving to hit the little yellow ball inside the white lines. She can be reached by email at BarbaraW@iKnowTennis.com

www.ingramcontent.com/pod-product-compliance
Lightning Source LLC
Chambersburg PA
CBHW041223040426
42443CB00002B/69